Walker

Journey to TORINO

(Grades 1–3)

10 9 8 7 6 5 4 3 2 1

ISBN   1-58000-122-X

TCR   3421

DIRECTOR OF OPERATIONS . . . . Robin L. Howland
PROJECT MANAGER . . . . Bryan K. Howland
WRITERS . . . . Greg Camden, M.A., and Eric Migliaccio
EDITOR. . . . . Sara Connolly
COVER DESIGNER . . . . Brenda DiAntonis
ART PRODUCTION MANAGER . . . . Kevin Barnes
ILLUSTRATOR . . . . Vicki Frazier
IMAGING . . . . James Edward Grace

Published in association with
and distributed by:

Griffin Publishing Group

18022 Cowan, Suite 202
Irvine, CA 92614
www.griffinpublishing.com

Teacher Created Resources, Inc.

6421 Industry Way
Westminster, CA 92683
www.teachercreated.com

Manufactured in the United States of America

Table of Contents

The Torino 2006 Olympic Winter Games

The air has grown cold, and ice and snow are all over the ground. After four long years, the time has come again. The world's greatest athletes are arriving in the Italian town of Torino to compete in the Olympic Winter Games.

Before each athlete began his or her journey toward Torino, he or she first had to start with the basics. Before the figure skaters could leap and spin, they had to take that first step onto the slick ice. Before the snowboarders could twist and soar, they had to first learn to stand.

Before we leave for Torino, it's time for you to show what you know about Italy and the Olympic Winter Games. In the spaces below, write words and/or draw pictures to show what you know.

Things to Think About

* foods of Italy

* customs of Italy

* events in the Olympic Winter Games

* who competes in the Olympic Winter Games

Italy	Olympic Winter Games

Look Inside "Olympians"

The word "Olympians" comes from the Greek language. That is because the Olympic Games began a long time ago in Olympia, Greece.

There are nine letters in the word "Olympians." You can spell a lot of other words just by using those nine letters. Complete the sentences below. Use only words that are spelled with the letters in "Olympians."

O	L	Y	M	P	I	A	N	S

1. Kristen used a ___ ___ ___ to clean up the spilled milk on the floor.

2. The policeman had a mustache above his ___ ___ ___.

3. I went to the park with ___ ___ best friend, Ben.

4. The woman put a quart of ___ ___ ___ in her car to make it run better.

5. Grandma took a small ___ ___ ___ from her cup of hot tea.

6. It's easy to ___ ___ ___ ___ and fall if you step on a banana peel.

Can you think of more words that can be spelled from the letters in the word "Olympians"? Write them down here.

Making and Using Olympic Mini-Books

Mini-books are a great way to introduce your students to the history of Olympic Winter Games. Follow the direction below to use "The First Olympic Winter Games Mini-Book" (pages 6 and 7) and "Olympic Winter Games Sports Mini-Book" (pages 8–10) with your students.

Materials Needed

* copies of "The First Olympic Winter Games Mini-Book" (pages 6 and 7)

* copies of "Sports of the Olympic Winter Games Mini-Book" (pages 8–10)

* scissors

* glue

* stapler

* two precut 4" x 5" (10 cm x 12.5 cm) sheets of construction paper for each book

Directions

1. Distribute the mini-book pages and have students cut them apart.

2. Direct students to glue the cover pages to one piece of construction paper.

3. Tell students to organize the book pages in sequential order, putting the extra piece of construction paper first. This will serve as the mini-books' cover.

4. Be sure the students have their pages in the correct order. Staple each book once in the top left-hand corner.

5. Have students add their names to their front covers.

6. Allow time for the students to color the pictures.

Uses

Use the books for independent reading or in reading groups.

The First Olympic Winter Games Mini-Book

The 1924 Olympic Winter Games

1.

The first Olympic Winter Games were held in 1924 in France.

2.

Over 250 athletes competed. Most were men. Only 13 women took part.

3.

An American speed skater won the first ever Olympic Winter Games gold medal.

4.

The First Olympic Winter Games
Mini-Book *(cont.)*

A ski jumper from Norway won three gold medals.

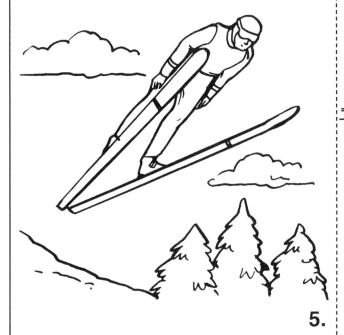

5.

The ice hockey team from Canada was very good. No team came close to beating them.

6.

An 11-year-old figure skater named Sonja Henie was the youngest person to compete.

7.

The 1924 Olympic Winter Games were a great idea! They still play them today.

8.

Sports of the Olympic Winter Games Mini-Book

Sports of

the Olympic

Winter

Games

1.

Athletes who compete in the Olympic Winter Games play many sports.

2.

Some athletes are figure skaters. They have to be graceful.

3.

Some athletes are speed skaters. They have to have strong legs.

4.

Sports of the Olympic Winter Games Mini-Book *(cont.)*

Some athletes are Alpine skiers. These athletes travel very fast down snow slopes.

5.

Some athletes are Nordic skiers. Some ski very far. Others jump off big ramps and fly through the air.

6.

Some athletes are snowboarders. They jump off ramps. They twist and spin and turn in the air.

7.

Some athletes are ice hockey players. They help their teammates put the puck in the goal.

8.

Sports of the Olympic Winter Games Mini-Book *(cont.)*

Some athletes are curlers. They try to roll an object onto a bulls-eye target.

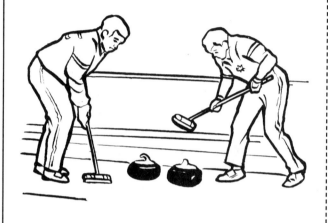

9.

Some athletes ride in a bobsled. They slide fast down an icy course.

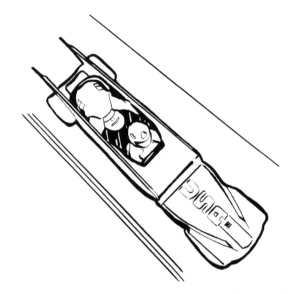

10.

Some athletes are lugers. A luge is like a sled.

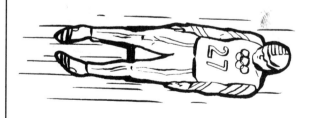

11.

All athletes hope to win a gold medal. Silver medals and bronze medals are good, too!

12.

Sports to Sort

Look at the cards below. Follow the directions. Then answer the questions.

* Find the equipment that skiers use. Color them green.

* Find the equipment that hockey players use. Color them red.

* Find the equipment that neither skiers or hockey players use. Draw a big **X** through them.

Which sport has the most cards? _____

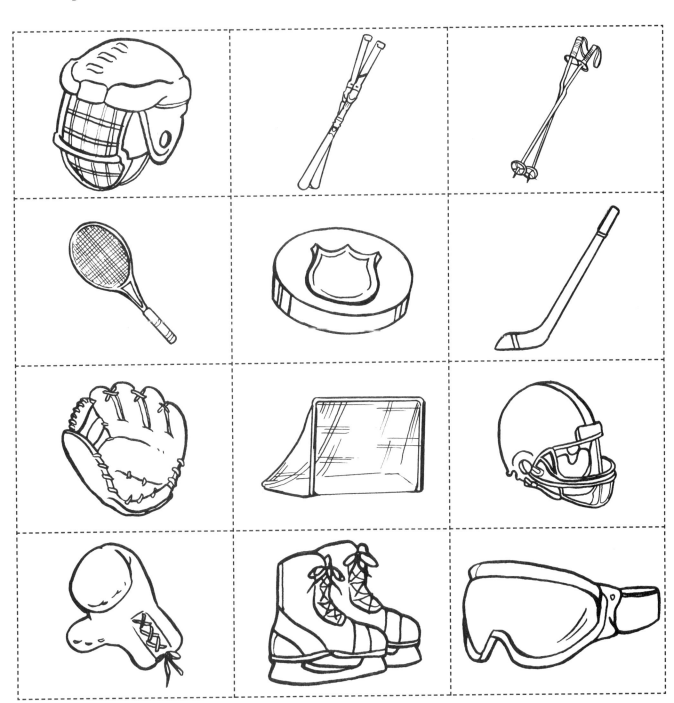

The Olympic Creed

Athletes do their best to follow the Olympic Creed. This is what the Olympic Creed says:

> *"The most important thing in the Olympic Games is not to win, but to take part, just as the most important thing in life is not the triumph but the struggle. The essential thing is not to have conquered but to have fought well."*

This is a good lesson for life. You can always be proud of yourself if you work hard and do your best.

Think about the things you do every day. Complete these sentences:

Yesterday I did my best _____

_____

Today I will do my best _____

_____

Tomorrow I will do my best _____

_____

Draw a picture of you doing your best.

Welcome to Torino

The 2006 Olympic Winter Games will be held in the city of Turin. Turin is in the country of Italy. In fact, the people of Italy call Turin by the name *Torino*. The city that hosts the Olympic Winter Games is called the host city.

Over 1.5 million people will visit Torino during the time of the Olympic Winter Games. They will need places to sleep and eat. They will need ways to get around the town. Being a host city is a lot of work!

What kinds of things do you think a host city needs to have for its visitors? Write five ideas here.

1. _____
   _____

2. _____
   _____

3. _____
   _____

4. _____
   _____

5. _____
   _____

Would the town you live in be a good host city for the Olympic Winter Games?

Why or why not? _____

_____

_____

_____

Host Countries

Italy is the host country of the 2006 Olympic Winter Games. Only 10 countries have had the honor of hosting the Olympic Winter Games. They are listed in the Country Box. In the boxes below, write the countries in alphabetical order.

Country Box			
France	Germany	Italy	Yugoslavia
Switzerland	Norway	Austria	Canada
United States		Japan	

United States

Italy

France

Switzerland

Japan

Canada

Germany

Austria

Norway

Yugoslavia

Country Shapes

The 2006 Olympic Winter Games will be played in
Italy. Have you ever seen a map of Italy? See the
picture to the right? That is what Italy looks like,

Doesn't it look just like a boot?

Are any other countries shaped like shoes or animals
or anything else? Look at the country shapes below.
On the lines below each shape, tell what you think
the country looks like. Use your imagination!

1. **United States**

_____

_____

2. **Cyprus**

_____

_____

3. **Newfoundland**

_____

_____

4. **France**

_____

_____

The Torch Relay

The torch for the Torino 2006 Olympic Winter Games has a curvy design. It is made of wood and metal. People from all over the world will get a chance to run with the Olympic torch. Then, one very special athlete gets to use the torch to light the Olympic flame. When this happens, the Olympic Winter Games have begun!

If you could choose, who do you think should light the Olympic flame? Choose a person you know or someone famous who you admire. Write that person's name and draw or paste in his or her picture. Then tell why you think he or she should be the one to light the Olympic flame.

person's name

picture

The Olympic Flag

The Olympic flag has five rings on it. Each ring is a different color. Each color represents a different part of the world:

❋ North and South America

❋ Europe

❋ Asia

❋ Africa

❋ Australia

The rings are blue, yellow, black, green, and red. Did you know that every flag in the world contains at least one of those colors?

On the flag below, color the rings as shown.

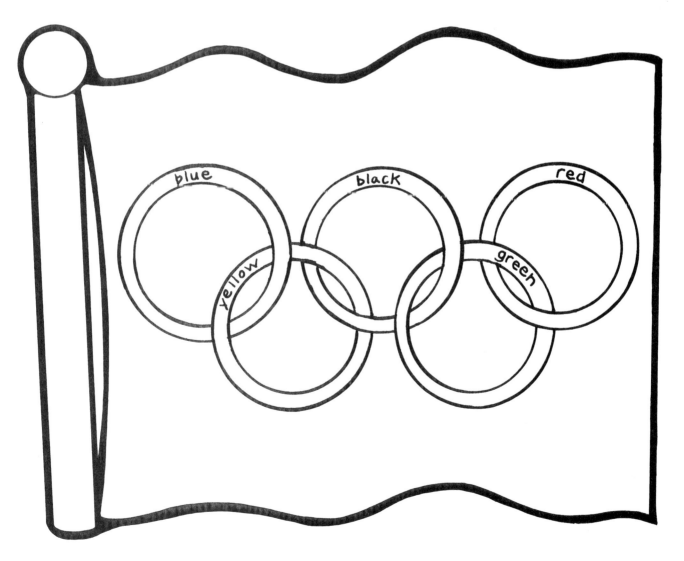

Making a Mascot

Olympic Winter Games mascots represent the host city and country in some way. Gliz and Neve are the mascots for the Torino 2006 Olympic Winter Games. Gliz is a playful ice cube, and Neve is a friendly snowball.

Think about the city where you live or a city that you know well. What makes it a special place? Write the name of the city on the line. Then draw a mascot for the city.

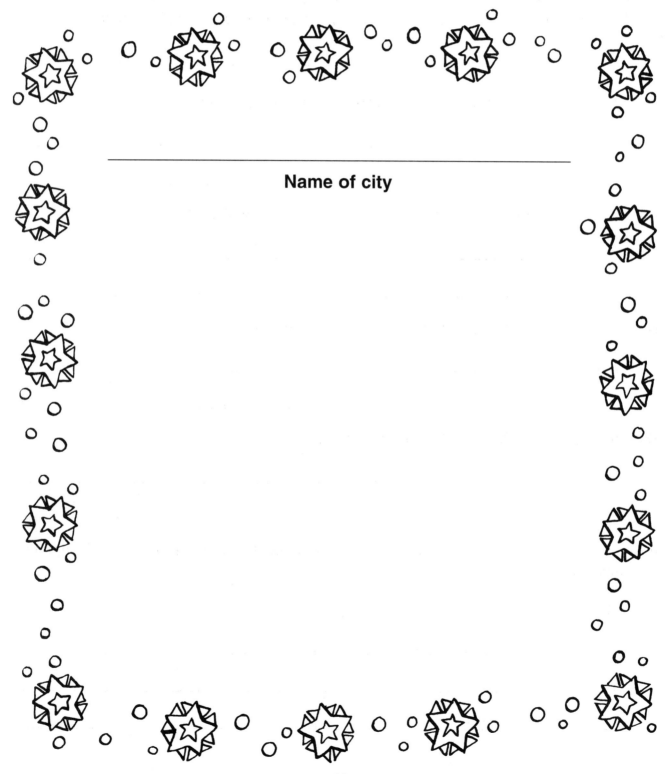

_____

Name of city

The Olympic Oath

An oath is a promise. All Olympic Winter Games athletes make an oath to play fair. Here are the words in the Olympic Oath:

> *In the name of all competitors, I promise that we shall take part in these Olympic Winter Games, respecting and abiding by the rules which govern them, in the true spirit of sportsmanship, for the glory of the sport and the honor of our team.*

Why do you think it is important to follow the rules of a sport?

_____

_____

Tell one way you in which you follow rules in sports or games.

_____

_____

Tell one way in which you follow rules in the classroom.

_____

_____

Tell one way in which you follow rules at home.

_____

_____

Write an oath that will help you to follow rules in the classroom or at home. Complete this sentence:

I promise _____

_____

_____

_____.

Olympic Pictograms

Make several copies per student of the Olympic Pictograms cards on page 21 and cut them out along the dotted lines. (You may want to laminate them for greater durability.) Use them for a variety of activities. Here are some ideas:

❋ Students can alphabetize the cards.

❋ Pairs of students can use the cards to play an Olympic version of "Go Fish."

❋ Pairs of students can use the cards to play an Olympic version of "Concentration." To play, give each pair of students two copies of each of the nine Olympic Pictograms cards. Have students place all 18 cards facedown. Player 1 turns over one card, and then turns over another. If the two cards are identical, Player 1 picks up the pair and goes again. If the two don't match, Player 1 returns both cards to the facedown position, and it is Player 2's turn. Continue until all pairs have been located.

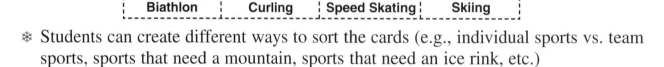

Biathlon   Curling   Speed Skating   Skiing

❋ Students can create different ways to sort the cards (e.g., individual sports vs. team sports, sports that need a mountain, sports that need an ice rink, etc.)

❋ Have the students place the cards facedown in a pile. Working in pairs, have students take turns picking one card at a time. Each student then shares everything he or she knows about that sport. When finished, the partner can add any details that may have been left out.

❋ While the Olympic Winter Games are in progress, use the cards as part of an Olympic-medals class chart. Place them on a bulletin board or large sheet of paper and record medal winners next to the corresponding sport.

❋ Create a Sports Equipment Chart. On a bulletin board or large sheet of paper, make nine columns. At the top of each column, place a different Olympic Pictograms card. Underneath each sport's logo, have students brainstorm the equipment that each sport requires.

❋ Let the students select a card to use as a visual story starter. Younger children can write three things they like about that sport and three things they don't like. Older students may want to create a fictional story about a child their age involved in that sport.

❋ Have your students create their own unique activity to share with the class.

Olympic Pictograms *(cont.)*

Cut out the Olympic Pictograms on the dotted lines. See page 20 for ways to use these pictograms in the classroom.

Biathlon	**Curling**	**Ice Hockey**
Bobsled	**Figure Skating**	**Luge**
Skiing	**Snowboarding**	**Speed Skating**

The Olympic Program

The Olympic Program is like a calendar. It shows when certain events will take place during the Olympic Winter Games. The Games will begin on February 10, 2006, and they will last until February 26, 2006.

A part of the Olympic Program is shown here. A checkmark (✔) means that the event will be played on that day.

	Sun	Mon	Tue	Wed	Thu	Fri	Sat
	12	13	14	15	16	17	18
Biathlon		✔	✔		✔		✔
Curling		✔	✔	✔	✔	✔	✔
Ice Hockey	✔	✔	✔	✔	✔	✔	✔
Snowboard	✔	✔			✔	✔	

Use the calendar to answer the following questions. Circle the correct answer.

1. How many days are shown on this calendar?

   5 days   **7 days**   **8 days**

2. Which of these sports is played on the most days?

   curling   **ice hockey**   **snowboarding**

3. Which of these sports is played on the least days?

   curling   **ice hockey**   **snowboarding**

4. On which of these days is every sport played?

   Wednesday   **Thursday**   **Friday**

5. Which of these sports is not played on Wednesday?

   biathlon   **curling**   **ice hockey**

Who Plays What?

Four athletes are getting ready to compete in the Olympic Winter Games. Can you guess which sport each one plays? Read the clues to learn what type of athlete each person is.

Clues

❄ Sarah likes to score goals.

❄ Derek goes around a track.

❄ Johnny and Sarah both wear skates.

Put an **X** in each box that can't be true. Put a ✓ in each box that is true.

	Ice Hockey Player	Figure Skater	Snowboarder	Speed Skater
Sarah				
Derek				
Gretchen				
Johnny				

Based on the clues, you can tell that . . .

1. Sarah is a(n) _____

2. Derek is a(n) _____

3. Gretchen is a(n) _____

4. Johnny is a(n) _____

Olympic Story Starters

Choose one of the following writing prompts to write a story about the Olympic Winter Games. Cut out the prompt on the dotted lines and paste it in the Story Box below. Then write your story.

My favorite Olympic Winter Sport is

If I made a new winter sport it would be

If I were an Olympic athlete, I would

Athletes wear special clothing because

If I went to Italy, I would see

Story Box

_____

_____

_____

_____

_____

_____

_____

_____

Blocks of Ice

Answer the following questions. Then find each answer in a block of ice below.   Color in the block containing that answer.

1. A _____ _____ _____ _____ is a type of sled.

2. The First Olympic Winter Games were held in the country of

   _____ _____ _____ _____ _____ _____.

3. In curling, players use _____ _____ _____ _____ _____ _____ to sweep the area in front of the stone.

4. The athlete who comes in second place wins the

   _____ _____ _____ _____ _____ _____ medal.

5. A special _____ _____ _____ _____ _____ is used to light the Olympic Flame during the Opening Ceremonies.

Which two blocks of ice have not been colored in? Use the words from the uncolored blocks to answer this question:

Two things that are needed for the Olympic Winter Games are

_____ _____ _____ and _____ _____ _____ _____.

Mathematical Matching

Complete the math problem in each box on the left. Each answer will be equal to the number of things described in the boxes on the right. Draw a line to match answers. The first one has been done for you.

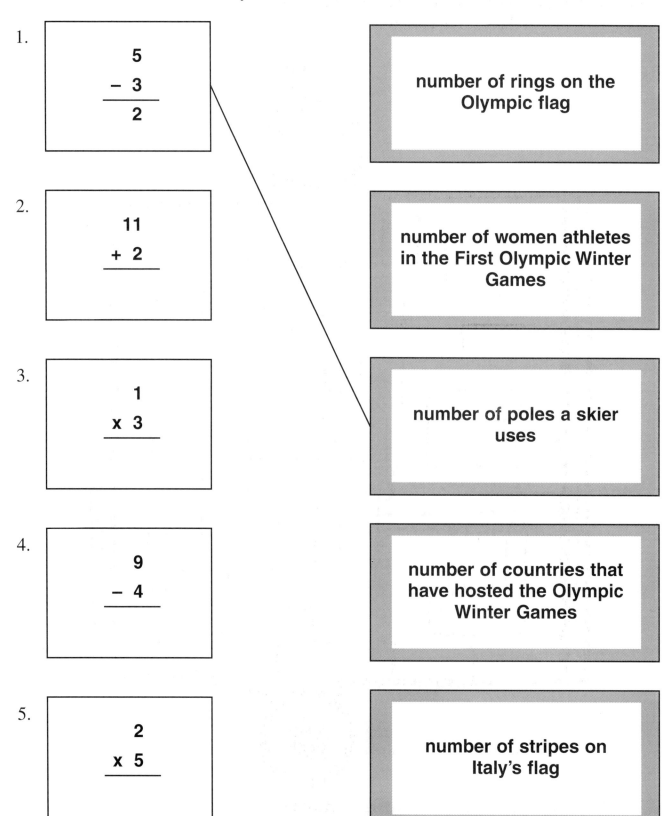

1.
$$\begin{array}{r} 5 \\ -\ 3 \\ \hline 2 \end{array}$$

number of rings on the Olympic flag

2.
$$\begin{array}{r} 11 \\ +\ 2 \\ \hline \end{array}$$

number of women athletes in the First Olympic Winter Games

3.
$$\begin{array}{r} 1 \\ \times\ 3 \\ \hline \end{array}$$

number of poles a skier uses

4.
$$\begin{array}{r} 9 \\ -\ 4 \\ \hline \end{array}$$

number of countries that have hosted the Olympic Winter Games

5.
$$\begin{array}{r} 2 \\ \times\ 5 \\ \hline \end{array}$$

number of stripes on Italy's flag

To the House

In curling, players try to slide the stone into the house. The stone looks a bit like a tea kettle. The house is a big bulls-eye target.

Now it's your turn to try and put the stone in the house. Find your way through the maze below to win the gold in curling.

Stone

House

Search and Sort

Figure Skating and Speed Skating

Can you find figure skating and speed skating words in the word search below? Use the words in the **Word Box** to help you.

Word Box			
COSTUME	JUMPS	SKATES	RINK
ICE	SUIT	SPINS	TRACK

T	O	L	S	Y	M	P	I	C
R	I	N	U	M	J	M	P	S
A	R	L	I	V	U	W	R	O
C	O	S	T	U	M	E	I	V
K	N	U	I	S	P	I	N	S
S	K	A	T	E	S	N	K	T
T	Q	U	E	R	I	C	E	E

Now sort the words from the word search. Use the Venn diagram below. Write the words from the sport of figure skating onto the box that says "Figure Skating," and the words from the sport of speed skating on the box labeled "Speed Skating." Place the words that are from both sports in the sections that is labeled "Both."

Figure Skating	Both	Speed Skating

The Path to 2006

Help this skier make it to the Torino 2006 Olympic Winter Games. He has three ski slopes to choose from. But only one of the slopes has numbers that add up to 2006.

* ❄ Color the slope **gold** that adds up to 2006.

* ❄ Color the other two slopes **green**.

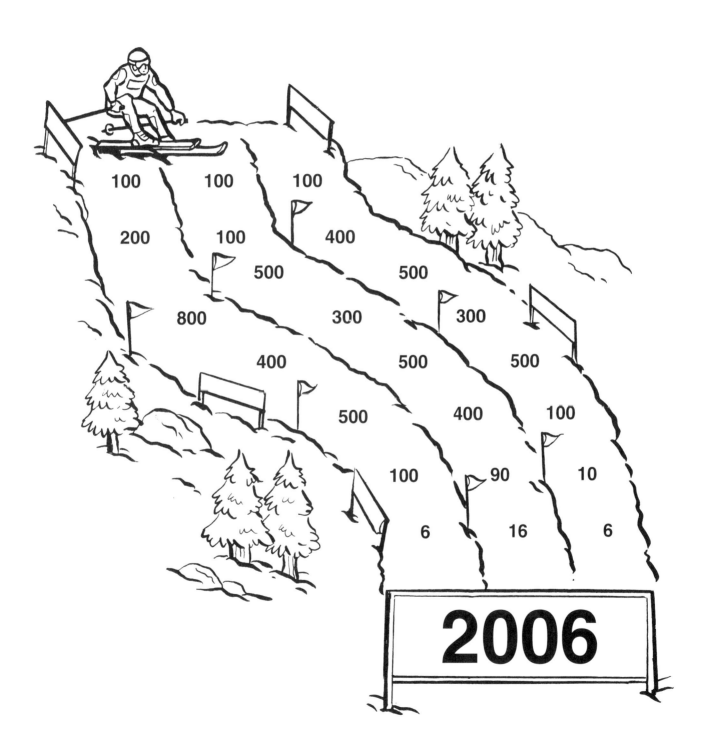

Sports Values

Look at the **Value Key**. Each letter has been given a number of points. Add the number of each letters in the sports words to find out the total number of points in the word. The first one has been done for you.

	Value Key		
A = 1	E = 5	K = 9	R = 13
B = 2	G = 6	L = 10	S = 14
C = 3	H = 7	N = 11	U = 15
D = 4	I = 8	O = 12	Y = 16

1.   L   U   G   E

  _10_ + _15_ + _6_ + _5_ =

$\boxed{36}$

2.   S   K   I   I   N   G

  ____ + ____ + ____ + ____ + ____ + ____ =

$\boxed{}$

3.   H   O   C   K   E   Y

  ____ + ____ + ____ + ____ + ____ + ____ =

$\boxed{}$

4.   B   O   B   S   L   E   D

  ____ + ____ + ____ + ____ + ____ + ____ + ____ =

$\boxed{}$

5.   C   U   R   L   I   N   G

  ____ + ____ + ____ + ____ + ____ + ____ + ____ =

$\boxed{}$

Bonus: Which word added up to the most points? _____

Reach for the Gold

See if you can take home the gold medal. For each question, the answer is given to you—but it's all scrambled up! Unscramble the dark letters to answer questions about the 2006 Olympic Winter Games.

1. A luger steers with his or her legs, shoulders, or **adhe**. ____ ____ ____ ____

2. A bobsledder wears a **metleh** to protect his or her head.

   ____ ____ ____ ____ ____ ____

3. The biathlon combines skiing and **nigthoos**.

   ____ ____ ____ ____ ____ ____ ____ ____

4. The fastest skiing event is called **nohdwill** skiing.

   ____ ____ ____ ____ ____ ____ ____ ____

5. Italy is on the continent of **peErou**. ____ ____ ____ ____ ____ ____

6. There are two main snowboarding events: the slalom and the **pifehalp**.

   ____ ____ ____ ____ ____ ____ ____ ____

- -

How did you do? Color in the medal that you earned and write your name in the space below.

Answer all 6 questions correctly = You are the best! The gold medal is yours!

Answer 4 or 5 questions correctly = Wow! You are a silver medal winner!

Answer 2 or 3 questions correctly = Congratulations! You have earned the bronze.

Answer 1 question correctly = Time to train for the next Olympic Winter Games.

Silver   Gold   Bronze

Answer Key

Page 4: Look Inside "Olympians"
1. mop
2. lip
3. my
4. oil
5. sip
6. slip

Page 11: Sort the Sports

hockey equipment: mask, puck, stick, goal, skates

skiing equipment: skis, poles, goggles

other equipment: tennis racket, football helmet, baseball glove, boxing glove

Page 14: Host Countries

in alphabetical order: Austria, Canada, France, Germany, Italy, Japan, Norway, Switzerland, United States, Yugoslavia

Page 22: The Olympic Program
1. 7 days
2. ice hockey
3. snowboarding
4. Thursday
5. biathlon

Page 23: Who Plays What?
1. Sarah is an ice hockey player.
2. Derek is a speed skater.
3. Gretchen is a snowboarder.
4. Johnny is a figure skater.

Page 25: Blocks of Ice
1. luge
2. France
3. brooms
4. silver
5. torch

box answers: ice and snow

Page 26:
1. 2 = poles a skier uses
2. 13 = women athletes in the First Olympic Winter Games
3. 3 = stripes on Italy's flag
4. 5 = rings on the Olympic flag
5. 10 = countries that have hosted the Olympic Winter Games

Page 27: To the House

Page 28: Search and Sort

T	O	L	S	Y	M	P	I	C
R	I	N	U	M	J	M	P	S
A	R	L	I	V	U	W	R	O
C	O	S	T	U	M	E	I	V
K	N	U	I	S	P	I	N	S
S	K	A	T	E	S	N	K	T
T	Q	U	E	R	I	C	E	E

Figure Skating: costume, ice, jumps, rink, skates, spins

Speed Skating: ice, skates, suit, track

Both: ice, skates

Page 29: The Path to 2006

The middle path adds up to 2006.

Page 30: Sports Pointers
1. Luge = 36
2. Skiing = 56
3. Hockey = 52
4. Bobsled = 49
5. Curling = 66

Bonus: Curling

Page 31: Reach for the Gold
1. head
2. helmet
3. shooting
4. downhill
5. Europe
6. halfpipe

Internet Research Sites

For more information on the Torino 2006 Olympic Winter Games, visit the following websites:

❋ www.torino2006.org

❋ www.usolympicteam.com

❋ www.olympic.org